*For all the Jewish refusenik-mothers
who want to live and bring up their Jewish children
in their homeland, Israel.*

Cover design: Irena Bat-Zvi

Publishing Editor: Vladimir Glozman.

Layout: Andrei Reznitzky

ISBN 965 – 314 – 000 – 0

A Child in Refusal: A Selection of articles
by refusenik-mothers and a lighthearted but
yet sad children's view of refusenik life.

A CHILD IN REFUSAL

Jerusalem
1985

ACKNOWLEDGEMENTS

Thanks must go to all the mothers and children both still in the Soviet Union and those fortunate few who were lucky enough to be released, for compiling this selection of articles and jokes.

We are most grateful to the Tsyrlin family for both creating the idea and the reality of the Jewish Kindergarten. Without their help this book would not have been possible.

The translation was gratefully performed by Shmuel Benmor. The typing was speedily carried out by Yael and the proof-reading by Sylvia and Angie. Many thanks to Maya Nemkovskaya for her help and to all those people who cooperated in producing the English version of this Russian text.

Josef Mendelevitch
Chairman of SJIEC

Shmuel Azarkh
Director of SJIEC

Dear Friends,

Many of you have most probably heard that in the Soviet Union there are quite a few Jewish refuseniks; that is to say, Jews who are denied by the Soviet authorities the possibility to immigrate to the country which we consider our homeland: Israel.

The problem of emigration from the USSR has already existed for a long time. This problem is discussed one way or another by politicians and communal organizations. Journalists write about this problem and the Soviet authorities resolve this problem in their own way. But we, women-refuseniks, want to show yet another aspect of this problem:the "refusenik child".

How do children growing up in refusenik families perceive these things? How do they differ from other children? What difficulties do they encounter? How do the children themselves feel and evaluate their position as refuseniks? These and several other questions we asked ourselves, our friends and acquaintances. It turned out that we have many problems in common for which we cannot always find a satisfactory solution. Occasionally, our opinions on a particular question have differed sharply.

We are offering you the opportunity to become more closely acquainted with several children of refuseniks who live in Moscow and to listen to what the mothers, as well as the children, have to say.

★ ★ ★

We previously sent a letter to Nancy Reagan in which we briefly stated our problems. It would appear appropriate to restate this here:

Dear Mrs. Reagan:

We are women whose families were refused permission to emigrate to Israel. It was with a feeling of excitement that we read in the July copy of the magazine, "America", about your sympathy and care for sick Korean children. Can there be a more noble task than to guard the health and happiness of children?

We want to confide to you the problems involved in the upbringing and education of our children. They are subject to ailments no less dangerous than physical illness. The normal system of a child is too fragile to cope with the hardships facing families of Refuseniks. At first sight their lives may seem normal, they have parents who do their best to provide for their care and education. They do not suffer from poverty or starvation, but their lives are full of hard problems and questions for which there are no answers. We have been trying to receive, from the authorities, permission to leave for Israel. In connection with this, our lives have stopped at this stage of anticipation. Our suspense has lasted for years. Our children experience the same overwhelming feeling of uncertainty and fear. They have lived a double life since the most tender age. On the one hand, the family brings them up through the Jewish tradition. On the other hand, the same devotion to tradition may cause misunderstanding or sneers and quite commonly open hostility. They are called names, they are called "fascists": Israel, the country they consider their mother is demeaned. There have been occasions on which our children were severely beaten. A Jewish child wearing a skullcap, missing classes on Saturday, saying a prayer before eating bread, is ostracized from the administration, teachers, and classmates. Our children turn to their mothers for protection each time they see a militia man on the street. They are afraid of the militia because they have been present at searches when their homes were turned upside down, where books and record cassettes were taken away; or even some of the family, those close and dear to them were arrested. We could go on enumerating on the hard suffering which befalls our children.

The bitter irony of our situation is that all of our problems can be solved quickly and easily. We turn to you hoping that our problems will find a response in your heart. It is so important for us to know that there are people in the world who care and are ready to help us.

Signed: Glozman, Gurevich, Shachovskaya, Yoffe, Dashevskaya, Sorina, Zanskaya, Litvak, Chernobilskaya, Kosharovskaya, Gorelick, Ginis, Edelshtein, Weinshtock, Khasina, Yasmina, Klotz, Ivanovska, Braginskaya, Shenina, Apter, Koppelmans, Shachovskaya, Matlina, Yoffe.

Olga Yoffe

WE AND OUR CHILDREN

We are the generation born at the end of the forties and the start of the fifties. Our childhood took place during a relatively quiet period, once the Stalinist anti-semitism which our parents experienced had already come to an end. We all (or nearly all) grew up in assimilated Jewish families, where not only did they not observe the Jewish tradition, but even the very word "Jew" they tried not to pronounce, replacing it instead with the idiom "Fifth point" (5th point in the Soviet internal passport is one's nationality – Jew). Many of us heard this phrase Zhid or Jew for the first time on the street. We rushed to our parents for explanations but they hardly understood what this meant. For them, their Judaism was connected with elders who were living out their last days, their grandmothers and grandfathers who were still holding onto their Tallit and Talmud and speaking Russian with a provincial accent.

"We are like everyone else," they believed and convinced us of this, if not by their words then by their style and way of life. And we believed them. But for some reason or another, it was sometimes inappropriate to mention one's surname aloud among not-so-close friends, or when filling in the nationality clause for class registration forms, we half covered the paper from our classmates' view. In a word, the usual ghetto mentality, as we now understand it.

But time passed, things changed around us, and we, too, changed. Life itself compelled us to find a different solution to this problem: "We are not like everyone else." Each one of us

10

came to his own understanding of this truth by a not so easy path.

Now we ourselves are parents, and the question has arisen as to how we should bring up our children. Obviously not as we were instructed! A child must not only know that he is a Jew but also be a Jew. We who have only recently begun to relate to Jewish spiritual values, are doing everything that is in our power to ensure that the word "Jew" is full of meaning for the child.

Our children speak and read Hebrew, sing Hebrew songs. They know who Abraham, Isaac and Jacob were. They remember that "we were slaves in Egypt," and together with us, they hope: "Next Year in Jerusalem!"

And when two and a half year-old Mark says, "I don't have a locomotive, but it doesn't matter I'm a Jew," or when seven year-old Rina replies to the insult "filthy Jew," with "I am a Jewess but in no way filthy," we, as their parents , experience justifiable feelings of pride.

We are content: our children do not resemble us. But, it is still true that the teaching of Hebrew is forbidden in the Soviet Union. But we instill in the child: "Each person must speak in his native tongue – a Russian in Russian, a Georgian in Georgian and a Jew, of course, in Hebrew. But don't tell to anyone where we meet for classes. And don't discuss it on the telephone. But you understand..." And, unfortunately, he does understand. He has already truly acquired his own sad experience in life.

He recalls when some unknown people broke into the apartment, acting as a children's kindergarten. They searched for something; they siezed something and asked the children, "What's your mother's name, your father's name?" and then, "Why was the kindergarten moved to a different flat" and more... and more... And so the child begins to understand that it is a little bit frightening to be a Jew and that one cannot tell everyone about "our affairs." And later on – school. And the 11 unavoidable political information classes where it is necessary to vilify Israel and Zionists. But we must keep quiet!

"That's impossible" – our good dear friends tell us, "a child is not capable of leading a dual life. Let him live like the rest while you are here, and when you leave, then..." But we do not know when that "then" will come about. In such families where the solution of this question is put off until "then", parents have to mutter when the child appears, "Shhh, he doesn't know anything about it" (and of course he does!) and parents see that the spiritual link with the child is lost. By not allowing him into their life, they soon find that it is too late. He has his own type of life – a different type.

So does it mean that in our circumstances it is impossible to find a solution to this problem? Does every attempt to find a solution lead to a dead end?

At any rate, we are convinced that, although our approach is not an easy one, it is a reliable and proper one. When we sit around the festive Passover table and see the radiant and attentive faces of our children, we know that even if not we, then at least they, will be "Next Year in Jerusalem."

★ ★ ★

The Jewish Kindergarten was organized in Moscow in an urban city flat in autumn 1977 (on the initiative of the Tsyrlins) by the parents and their friends. There were then ten children in the Kindergarten. The children studied Hebrew, mathematics, Russian language, drawing, singing and they became acquainted with the history of the Jewish people.

In 1978, the Kindergarten was transferred to Bikovo where it lasted a year. At that time, the greatest problem for the staff/educators in the Kindergarten was the continual changing around of the children; scarcely had a child become accustomed to the Kindergarten when the child would leave for Israel. In 1980, the Tsyrlins themselves left for Israel but the Kindergarten continued to function. "From that moment onwards, we began to be persecuted," recalls **Katya Glozman:**

—We attempted to organize the children's way of life as well as possible but here we encountered the following types of difficulties: How is it possible to begin buying food for all the children when the queues in the shop are spitefully shouting and jealously counting each kilogram purchased by us? How can one go for a walk with the children if the local grandmothers grumble, "Yet again they have brought those Jewish children here. There's no room left in the playground for our poor grandchildren." We attempted to conduct lessons regularly but we lacked the skill, the means and the knowledge. But the main 13

**Festival in the Kindergarden flat near the Botanical
Gardens**

thing was that we passionately wanted the Kindergarten to exist. However, some officials were extremely unhappy about this; they were exasperated by the impudence of the Jews who wanted to raise their children in the Jewish traditional spirit; they began to extinguish the Kindergarten.

In the winter of 1980, a policeman from the local division came and asked what we were doing in this flat. As we had hired the flat officially, he could find no fault and went away. For some time we lived peacefully. Then the neighbors started to complain and then suddenly stopped. It was as if someone had incited the neighbors to complain and then lost interest in their protests.

We continued to live our life, to be happy looking at the children making merry at our festivals, learning by heart Jewish songs or putting together their first words in Hebrew. The children affectionately named our house "the Botanical Kindergarten" and every Monday, hurriedly climbed up the 13 floors by foot if the lift was not working. Each child had a lot to do: first of all, one had to take off one's coat and hang it up on the hook, and this is difficult if, from all sides your friends are fussing around and shouting "Dina's arrived!" One has to play with the construction kit before the lesson and one must leave it right before the lesson. There's a little to cry about (Mama's left) and to laugh about (Boris is pulling faces) and simply to consider oneself a happy child who has dear friends.

But all of this, it turns out, is impossible. It is impossible to come into this favorite house (which, it is said, has broken "the official sanitary regulations"), it is impossible to pacify them by listening to Jewish fables, by teaching cheerful songs by heart, by drinking fruit compote from one's favorite cup and by boasting who would be the best Esther at Purim.

But then "they" arrived. The tiny children against the big "uncles". The children spin around from the clicking camera, clinging one to another and looking inquisitively. "Have bandits broken in?" We are ordered to evacuate the flat.

But on the following Monday, we arrive all the same, not 15

willing to believe that everything is over. We stand, confused, looking at the door. The keyhole is covered with a paper with some print on it. Ilyusha's eyes are enraged. "Can we tear this paper to shreds?" Only with difficulty can we stifle this desire within ourselves. What is next? In order to divert the attention of the children, we take them to a children's café, but they cannot be calmed down. "Will we never again return to our Botanical Kindergarten?!" How can we comfort them, when we ourselves are experiencing exactly the same fear as they?

Having consulted among ourselves, we decided to go to different flats. We are required to split up the Kindergarten into two groups by age. The older group lives according to the following timetable: four days the children are with me, and the following Monday – at Rimma's, and so on, each week. For the time being this plan holds. There are a whole host of difficulties: bedding here, bedding there, crockery here, crockery there. Books, toys, educational aids, we carry them all with us here and there. But – we are still alive! We will exist until the summer and then we will relax and think of something. The neighbors have already begun to complain, but we have got around it. And then the summer comes. We dismiss the Kindergarten for the holidays, and, troubled, we try to envisage how we can continue further. And then suddenly – what happiness! A possibility we have dreamed of for ages: a big house, a summer house, children in the fresh air the whole day, our little world (no one to persecute us), plenty of space, free and comfortable. We are full of enthusiasm and want to do everything here. Our fathers are helping us out with every bit of strength. They will not throw us out of here. Previously, it was a town flat, but here is a summer house. We can build everything in a big and proper way. We paint the beds; we fix lovely little hooks with pictures on for each child – so it is pleasant for our children. Lessons pass splendidly. The children are cheerful, the adults happy. At long last, we can give our children everything we wanted. Except, of course, Eretz Yisrael! But this will come. Then we will be able to bring up our children as real Jews. We are doing necessary work and receiving a colossal amount of satisfaction.

We are continually improving the summer house, introducing new classes and thinking up new amusements. All of this is so wonderful that when "it" occurs, no one can really comprehend. Again we have a visit from the "Bandits." They frightened the children; they frightened the life out of a frail woman; they stole books and ordered us to clear out. What self-control our children displayed when, on the next day, two black cars arrived to convince us that the cheerful hubbub of children in this house must not be heard.

This was a big blow for all of us. The youngest children were severely frightened; the older ones were already so traumatized that it took even more to calm them down.

And again, we are homeless. We do not want to – we cannot part. What can we do so that they will not drive us out again? It appears quite clear. They drive us out because we hired the flat. And if we install the Kindergarten in our own flat, then no one can do anything. Previously, they had not dared drive us out of our own or Rimma's flat!

We again set off for Rimma's flat. After our spacious dacha, two rooms are somewhat small for us. And there is none of the past zeal to create something here, as it is already understood that this flat is a temporary shelter. The children ask with alarm: "Won't the KGB come here?" We assure them, no, although we ourselves are uncertain of anything. What could be more scary than ghosts and witches?

Since our children have seen something frightening, they rush to avoid every passing policeman and never enter a lift if a moustached figure stands there. And we encourage them in this fear, convincing them not to speak to anyone about our Jewish Kindergarten, about our Hebrew and history lessons. But what we truly want is for the children to spend longer together and for "them" not to touch us.

However, we did not succeed in avoiding calamities. The children had to go through the fear of contact with the KGB yet another time. They behaved themselves with dignity. The older ones comforted the smaller ones and hid Judith Khassina because the KGB men for some reason or another wanted to know which is the daughter of Natasha Khassina.

On this occasion, we had to disperse to our homes. We could not fight with the KGB as we feared for the health and state of mind of our children.

Our children have grown up, have gone to school. New children have been born and again the parents face the question: whether or not to devote time and energy to the Jewish Kindergarten, realizing that on the one hand how beneficial this is for the children, but on the other hand, foreseeing everything that awaits their children.

IRA GINIS RELATES

Family has been in refusal 7 years. Three children: Yula (Freida) – 12, Alya (Brocha) – 10, and Ariel – 1.

When we gave in our application to leave for Israel, my elder daughter was 5 and the younger 3. This year we celebrate our first Bat Mitzvah, and the next one is not so far away. Our little girl is already 10.

It is hard to preserve any optimism after 7 years in refusal, but somewhere deep down inside, I hope, "G-d willing, we will celebrate the younger one's Bat Mitzvah in Israel. I cannot allow myself to hope for more than that. One must look at life clearly, and if one looks clearly, the main thing is fear – that endlessly returning thought: "What will become of us?"

During the years in refusal, a re-evaluation of values has taken place in our family. We have got rid of many illusions, obtained new ideals, new interests. Youth has been replaced by maturity and our children have grown up and learnt a lot. They have learnt to identify "us" and "them". They understand very well what one can say and where, and what one should not say. They even have acquired a working experience of this, something which not all adults can come to terms with. They have learnt to mix with the general group of children at school, whilst being outside this group and concealing from it the rest of their life. Is this good for them? Do they need these qualities? In the final analysis, Jews in the Diaspora were often forced to use them. But our children!...

And they and we live with one thought: that all of this is 19 temporary. But for how long? I am continually fearful for their future. Soon we shall have to think about a profession as one must orientate oneself around something, and to show them the way in life. But in what life?! And which way?!

We are deprived of the greatest parental happiness: that of seeing in our children the embodiment of our unrealized hopes, of giving them every possibility for a harmonious development. Our fate is crippled and the same fate threatens our children if we do not receive permission to leave in the near future. And our children sense that their parents are not all-powerful, that they are not in control of circumstances. And in their hearts a fear begins to develop – "And suppose we don't leave?"

Recently I gave birth to a son. We all were very happy. But time moves on so quickly. The child is already a year old, and I pray to G-d from morning to night that he shall never know the burden of life in the Diaspora.

The children of Ginis

LEAH CHERNOBILSKY RECOUNTS

Family 10 years in refusal. Anna – 14, Evgeny – 11, Yosef – 1.5. Father – a Prisoner of Zion, spent 1980-81 in a camp.

"Mama!" my ten year-old daughter recoils back from the window. "Police!"

I look out of the window. The two lads in police uniforms whom I sometimes see here are friends of our neighbors on the third floor. Why do their uniforms inspire such panic in the hearts of my children? With such a depressing fear why do they follow every police car which passes by or every passing policemen? Is he coming to our entrance?

It is because more than once these people smashed down our door, broke into the flat, turned everything upside down, swarming into things and books. KGB agents in plain clothes followed after them, or they were even dressed up in the same uniform. They led away papa, a man who could do everything, except defend his own home and children from these bandit-like invasions, and in the bitter awareness of his helplessness, could only throw out embitteredly, "Fascists!".

I saw how an eight year-old boy cried because the KGB agents took away a camera which he had received the day before as a birthday present. His parents comforted him. Maybe they will give it back?

"No," bitterly confirmed our son's five year-old girl friend, "they never give anything back!" This little girl had already experienced a difficult life. She had already learnt to make sad generalizations.

A four year-old mischievious boy, whilst enviously looking at a splendid large tower built from cubes by his older friends, maliciously promised, "The KGB man will come and will break your tower!"

That's how our children live. They believe in our ideals. They share with us not only our dreams about Israel, but also the burden of struggling for emigration and the sorrow of our failures and defeats.

When we began our struggle to leave, we had only two small ones. We dreamed of travelling to Eretz Yisrael, to build our country with everybody there and to create a happy future for our children. But after 10 years of refusal, our "little ones" have grown up and have become our "little friends" in this struggle, and they are as convinced Zionists as we are.

How difficult it is for our children to go to school where the teachers blacken and slander Israel, and demand similar behaviour from the pupils!

Nevertheless, our children are proud of their Judaism. They well understand what benefit the struggle to leave brings: some Jews happily leave for Israel, but others at the same time are beaten, are intimidated, are thrown behind bars. But the first group is the larger!

Yes, the children were greatly upset when Boris was imprisoned and since then, they still wake up in tears at night, tortured by nightmares. And when one family or another at long last receives permission to leave, the children find it very difficult to part, possibly for many years, with their friends. Our children would also like to leave for Eretz Yisrael.

Our children also see how parcels are collected for the "Prisoners of Zion." How everyone tries to help them and their families. And our children are convinced: better to live like this as we now do and to struggle, and to accompany friends on their way to Israel, than to be submissive, passive, "useful" Jews and remain here forever in a strange, hostile environment.

One day, my elder daughter told me that she recently had met with a "wonderful girl" among her group of friends. This girl told her about her parents. And my daughter became annoyed by having to keep silent.

"You know," she told me, "I told her that my parents are fighters. They live a very unusual life."

I got a little nervous. "You'll see that girl will retell her parents and they will advise her to stay clear of you."

And then I thought, our children too have an exceptional life, even if it is, at times, very difficult.

The fraternity of Jews gives them a happiness which we did not know in our childhood. Our parents taught us never to forget that we were Jews and that the hostile world around us could turn against us at any minute. Our children learn differently. Maybe it is difficult for us at present, extremely difficult for the Prisoners. But Jews throughout the world think about us and fight for us.

The wonderful feeling of solidarity cleanses and inspires our children's souls. We are certain: our children will have a happy life!

 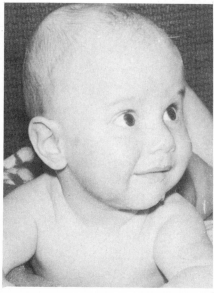

The children of Chernobilsky

Zoya Kopelman

WHAT NEEDS TO BE SAID ABOUT THE LIFE OF OUR CHILDREN IN REFUSAL

Our life in refusal has undoubtedly given us several advantages: we have become internally free and have acquired a feeling of national self-confidence. Our realization and the suffering for our desire to live in Israel has given us — a persecuted and wandering people — a feeling of homeland, of continuity of the generations, coming from the roots of our distant past.

But we are not yet on our way to Israel. They do not allow us out of the USSR. If someone's friends or close relatives are able to leave, the separation will last for years. Over the years in refusal, there has arisen a new generation of Jewish children, trying to speak Hebrew, learning by heart and singing Israeli songs and poems, revering their ancient G-d and awaiting the coming Sabbath, our religious and national holiday, with anticipation. They light candles at home where there is a freshly-baked smell of chalot, and all the family and friends with their children sit around an attractive table and sing in Hebrew the eternal words of the prayers and the psalms.

How wonderful, you say. Yet on Monday morning, our children are off to school where from the first to the last lesson they are instructed how they are required to behave according to the political information doctrines in which Israel is labelled as a fascist state and accused of never-ending evil acts against the peaceful Arab population. "Israeli soldiers", they tell the children (who understand, along with everyone else that this means "Jewish soldiers") "are killing and murdering, and the blood of their victims flows in Lebanon." The hearts of our children become enraged by the slander, because at home they hear a completely different story. But they must keep quiet and tolerate it all, because their parents never stop reminding them: silence. They are many; we are few, and what point in teaching them a lesson? But despite all this, sometimes a child whose parents are refuseniks will not be able to restrain himself. "Not true. Israel is not fascist!" Such a bold child will be ostracized, beaten and occasionally attacked brutally so that a long period of hospital treatment is needed.

How can we as parents resist the anti-Israel, and often openly anti-Semitic propaganda which is evident everywhere, in books, on television and radio? To raise our children as Jews, as future citizens of Israel, we are condemning them to isolation in the classroom and in the schoolyard. From a very early age, we require them to enter into a dual existence, depriving them of one of the most attractive characteristics of childhood: spontaneity.

My seven year-old daughter sits at home and is learning a story in Hebrew. The telephone rings. "What are you doing?" Grandma asks her. "I'm learning Heb..." The girl falls silent midway through the word and looks at me fearfully. She had forgotten that it is not allowed to speak about Hebrew lessons on the phone. It could lead to unpleasantness for mother and father. In the USSR, all study of Hebrew is forbidden, and in the best library in the country, the Lenin Library, all study literature in Hebrew is located in a closed section for which special permission to enter is needed. Hence it is not allowed to speak about Torah lessons on the telephone, as in the USSR the religious education of children is punishable in accordance with a special article of the Criminal Code. All prayerbooks and Bibles were either issued a long time ago or are from abroad. Why? Why is it impossible to buy a children's book in Hebrew? Why are there no kosher food items? Even without them, the undistinguishable assortment of foodstuffs in the shops is, for the religious Jews, becoming more and more scanty. Children

Avia Kopelman (7½ years old)
6 years in refusal.

become acquainted with the world, and they never tire of asking questions. As they grow up in refusal, the world around them seems unjust and illogical and, not infrequently, openly hostile.

Friends come to the parents and "serious talks" take place. In our small apartments, it is hard to divide up the space and the children hear the words "arrested," "picked up," "convicted." Who was arrested? For what was he convicted? They ask these questions later on. Since we do not want to hand over their souls to alien surroundings, we explain. A young man was arrested who had taught himself Hebrew and had taught the language to others who openly declared they wanted to leave for Israel.

I have become proud when to the standard question: "What will you become when you grow up?", my elder daughter invariably answers, "I will search for the key to the prisons and will release all the good people."

My daughter was then six years old.

Therefore, all Jewish people and people of good will throughout the world must combine their efforts and strive so that our lives in refusal should not be so long.

ROSA GORELICK SHARES HER THOUGHTS

A great deal of attention is paid to children throughout the world. Questions of infant mortality, child hunger, education, etc., are all sharply posed. Not a single thinking person, especially not a woman, can remain indifferent to these problems. Everyone wants to see laughing, playing, happy children. Each one of us, like any mother anywhere around the world, dreams of happiness for her children, and tries to do everything to ensure that her child will grow up healthy, clever and a complete person.

True – our children are not starving. They are dressed; they have a roof over their heads, and maternal warmth. But they also have their problems, which stem from our life in refusal which, even for an adult, is not easy to cope with. We, of course, are not doctors, not psychologists, and cannot evaluate fully or foresee all the after-effects of a dual life for the child's mind and body. But one doesn't need to be a specialist to see that all of this affects the child in a detrimental way. After all, it is well-known that the character of the child is formed in the early years as well as the basis for his/her outlook on the world.

We want them to grow up to be honest, just, but from their childhood they know that there are some people with whom they cannot say things which they can say openly with others, and that they must conceal a great deal. Thus our children learn to live.

We want to raise our children as free people, able to respect themselves and others. But from infancy, they begin to feel that they are different from the rest, they see that their family life differs from all the other surrounding families. How will all of this be expressed in the future? Possibly the child will decide that he is better than the rest and will grow up to be arrogant and unpleasant. Perhaps the opposite, the development of an inferiority complex, will be the case.

We want our children not only to love us but also to respect us. How can one speak about esteem when we cannot answer the main questions: "Why can one know Russian but not Hebrew? Why can we speak at home and not in the street? Why at the festival of Passover must our parents go to work and we to Kindergarten? And the main question: Why can we not leave for Israel? Why will they not let us go? Why?

What can we answer them? We ourselves ask the same question: Why do they keep us here? Why do they need us in this country? For what purpose is our fate to be sacrificed?

We look away from the bright, inquisitive eyes of our little ones as we give them indistinct, incomprehensible answers: "We have to wait. Now it is impossible. That's how it is..." And then the children remain alone with their questions. What do they think of us? "Our perents cannot answer us. Therefore, they cannot know everyyhig." They see our helplessness, that we cannot be support to them in every–thing. Do they not sense our defeselessness in an alien world (from a very early?)

Can our children really grow up calm, balanced and optimistic? We hope that our children will be physically strong and healthy, but for this, one must burden them a little. First of all, there must be a healthy, peaceful atmosphere at home. But our families live in a state of continual tension, in conditions of unabated stress with too wide a range of emotions – crazy hope to hopeless despair.

And surely our children sense all of this very clearly. Is it healthy for their developing nerves and mind to have all of this? Of course, every family has its problems, its complications. But it is one thing to find solutions to internal complications, and quite another to have one's life tied up with no possibility of changing it. The only thing left is to wait. But for how long? After all, the years are passing. Parents are growing old during the years of refusal. They are losing their optimism, their professions, their work.

Children are growing up. With each passing year, the questions about their futures become more urgent. The older the child, the harder it will be for him to adjust to a new place.

In a human sense, it all becomes more painful and insulting especially when we think of how easy it could be to solve all our problems. For what cause are we and our children suffering?

★ ★ ★

Twenty-one families took part in the compilation of this survey. Of these, there were six with three or more children. There were six children aged 0–3; fourteen children between 3–7; nineteen children of school age and two children above school age. The children, on the average, have spent five to seven years in refusal.

Children born in refusal:

1. **Judith Khasina**	– 8 years
2. **Dina Kopelman**	– 5 years
3. **Naomi Rakhlenko**	– 4.5 years
4. **Natan Kara-Ivanov**	– 4 years
5. **Ilana Litvak**	– 3.5 years
6. **Lisa Klotz**	– 3 years
7. **Ariel Yuzefovich**	– 2.5 years
8. **Dina Kara-Ivanov**	– 2 years
9. **Ariel Ginis**	– 1 year
10. **Anya Klotz**	– 1 year
11. **Leva Klotz**	– 1 year
12. **Joseph Chernobilsky**	– 6 months

From our conversations with the parents, we were able to draw several general conclusions which perhaps can be considered justified for a large percentage of refusenik families. Moreover, besides this, there appeared some interesting details and points on the lives of our children.

All the children know that they are Jews. As a rule, they either consider this natural or are proud of their Judaism. Only one child felt that "it was not good to be a Jew in this country."

Amongst the others, there were other such answers. The

mother of Mark and Yosef Gurvich said, "At first, the children thought that a Jew is one who speaks Hebrew. Then was added: one who has a G-d. Now they realize that there are Jews who have neither the language, nor G-d, like for example, grandma and grandpa, aunts and uncles."

The mother of Masha Braginsky tells that her daughter knows that she is a Jew. However, to explain to those around her what she understands by this was as difficult as trying to explain to a blind person what is daylight.

The mother of Dina Yoffe states, "My daughter can stand up for herself even if they tease her for being a Jew, and not feel wounded by this. It is true though, that one day she came home deeply shaken and upset because a five year-old boy had said that 'Jew' meant 'fascist.' "

Do the children know that the family is in refusal? Among the children who were old enough to realize this, only one did not know. Almost all the children fantasize over this situation and build fantastic plans. The Gurvich brothers compare their situation with the lives of the Jews in Egypt during Pharoah's time. Rina Fulmacht dreams that all the Jews will be gathered together in one house and then this house will develop wings and fly off to Israel.

About the existence of Hebrew and its special alphabet, all the children are aware. Twenty children study Hebrew, some are trying to compose short stories, poems and songs in Hebrew. In the families of Gurvich, Yuzefovich and Chernobilsky, one of the parents relates to the children only in Hebrew and the children speak in both languages.

Jewish holidays are observed in all the families. The children are told of the history of the Jewish people, and the children relate to this with great interest.

The mother of Simcha and Paulina Sorin says that the Jewish holidays have become family ones and that the children follow the calendar closely and wait for these days.

The Jewish legends serve them as a theme of discussion with the children and as a short story before sleep.

It turns out that the majority of children in refusal who attend state kindergartens and schools, adapt well externally, but all the same, not one of them has close friends there. Miriam Sud goes to kindergarten and wants the kindergarten to be full of Jewish children. She cannot understand why this is impossible.

Our children are not growing closer to their peers because they are afraid that unnecessary frankness will attract misunderstanding, alienation and open hostility. The children do not want to hear, as happened to Simcha Sorin, "Clear off to Israel!" Mark Yuzefovich, in general, prefers to mix with Russian children rather than with Jewish children who are embarrassed by their own Judaism. After all, you cannot explain to the latter a philosophy such as Zionism.

In our children's lives, there were open conflicts.

The mother of Mark Yuzefovich relates, "In the younger classes, Mark coped surprisingly well with what they told him at school and what he heard at home. Then he began to understand more and began to criticize things with which he did not agree. On one occasion, they organized "A Solidarity Fair." The children made different items and then sold them to their classmates. The money they received was sent to the "Peace Fund." At first, Mark was annoyed by the fact that if an item was not sold, the child had to buy his own creation. But when the teacher explained that the money gathered at the "Solidarity Fair" was to be used to buy arms for the Arab countries, Mark refused outright to participate in the "Fair." "I do not want this money to buy bombs which will be thrown at Israeli children!" he declared openly. Mark was accused of being devoid of patriotism, to which he answered that he was indeed a patriot, but added his own meaning to this concept. Then he was summoned to the gathering of the Pioneer Circle, who threatened to deprive him of his Pioneer tie. Then the director of the school and the teacher of history wrote to the KGB that Mark's father is "badly bringing up his son."

32   Dina Yoffe had only been in school one year but had already

adopted the position that we are here as guests and everything around us is alien because we never have our own lives. Dina's mother brings the following example to our attention: In the summer of 1985, there was an International Youth Festival in Moscow. The teacher warned the children, "Foreigners will be coming and will give gifts to the children which will explode". The reaction of Dina was, "Why does she lie all the time?!"

Many children have witnessed the arrival of the KGB in their homes. The immediate reaction of the children and the after-effects of such visits are the same for all: fear, horror, nightmares, hysterics and long-term depression. Judith and Aliona Khasina still experience a hatred for all those who are persecuting them. Ilana and Miriam Yuzefovich looked with hatred at the man who had played with them and then led a friend of the family away for questioning.

The mother of Mitya Klotz, together with nearly all the parents, notes that her son is frightened of policemen. This youngster's fear has not waned since the police unexpectedly appeared at the Jewish Kindergarten two years ago.

In conclusion, we want to quote the words of Ira Dashevsky, mother of three children: "In addition to the split personality with which we were raised, there has been added a feeling that we are being persecuted. On the other hand, the hope in G-d advantageously distinguishes their childhood from ours."

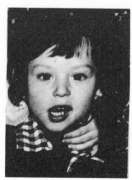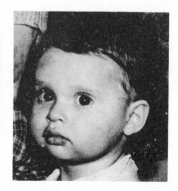

The children of Ira Dashevsky

OUR CHILDREN SPEAK

Dina Yoffe, 7 years old.

After watching a performance of "Blue Bird":

"Does the "Blue Bird" fly from one country to another?"

"Yes"

"And brings happiness?"

"Yes"

"Then I know that most of all she lives in Eretz Yisrael, as truly, the very happiest people live there."

Ariel Yuzefovich, *2½years old. Born in refusal.*

"Now we are living at the summer house and then we are going home."

"Home?"

"Well, yes, home to Israel, to grandmother."

Mark Yuzefovich, 5 years old.

"Grandma is so lucky. She can even lie in the Dead Sea and read a newspaper!"

Dina Kopelman, *5½ years old, born in refusal.*

Mother with enthusiasm:

"How much nicer it is to live here at the summer house than in Moscow!"

"But where, all the same, is it better? At the summer house or in Israel?"

The Gurviches chat with an assimilated relative about Israel:

Mark Gurvich, 7 years old.

"But you'll come to Israel, Uncle Vitya.

Yosef Gurvich, *6½ years old. (5 years in refusal)*

"Don't be afraid. Russians live there also!"

35

Dina Yoffe, *7 years old. 6 years in refusal.*

At the summer house:
"In Israel, are there mosquitoes?"
"I don't know. Why?"
"Because I don't want to be bitten by mosquitoes for the rest of my life."

★ ★ ★

"Mama, when will they let us go to Eretz Yisrael? Or otherwise let the Messiah come soon and then, we'll leave all the same."

Mark Yuzefovich, *11 years old. 5 years in refusal.*

Ilana: "Mama, is it true that there is a G-d?"

Mother: "I think so, yes."

Mark: "Then why up until now don't they let us leave for Eretz Yisrael?! We can't hold out any longer!"

Paulina Sorin, *5 years old, 4 years in refusal.*

Whilst learning the Passover song "Dayenu"

"And I've been to Egypt."

"When did you manage to spend time there?"

"Well, we were all there a long time ago!" (under influence of the Passover Haggadah.)

Miriam Sud, *4 years old,* together with mother at home on Shabbat.

"Mama, where's Papa?"

"He's gone to work."

"What, only Jewish *females* don't work on Shabbat?"

37

Ilya Sorin, *5 years old and* **Yosef Sorin,** *6 months old.*

Ilya, after hearing the Biblical story of Joseph and his brothers:

"Now that I have a brother, Joseph, I need a sister, Dina."

Pavel Praisman, 5 years old. During the preparation of this material the family received permission to emigrate and are now living in Jerusalem.

"Grandma, I'm leaving for Israel!"

"But what's that - Israel?"

"But really! How can you not know! It's that country from which both you and I were driven out from long ago."

Ilya Sorin, 5 years old.

With his grandfather, approaching a park. The gatekeeper, standing with his back to them, is closing the gate. Grandfather asks him to wait.

Ilya: "Grandpa, you are like G-d. That man doesn't see you but hears your voice!"

Dina Yoffe, 7 years old.

Discovering a Chanukah coin under her pillow one morning:

"What a great festival Chanukah is! Then, there was one large miracle but now there are many smaller ones."

Leah Finkelberg, *6 years old, 3 years in refusal.*

"Why did the Jews leave Egypt?"

"Because Pharoah dealt with them very badly."

"So why didn't they get rid of Pharoah?"

Ilana Yuzefovich, *6 years old, 5 years in refusal.*

"I know why boys have Bar-Mitzvah at 13 and why girls at 12."

"Why?"

"Because girls cannot hold out!"

★ ★ ★

Reading the warning on the washing machine:

"Mama, why can't you open the drum of the machine until it has stopped completely?"

"Because there will be a flood."

"How can you say that, Mama? G-d promised that there would never be another flood."

Miriam Yuzefovich, *9 years old, 3 years in refusal.*

"I love woodpeckers a lot, you know why? Because they have a yarmulka (kipa) on their heads."

★ ★ ★

"Mama, B'nei Yisrael's honor, I won't do it again!"

40

Mark Yuzefovich, 7 years old.
Looking at the sculpture by Michaelangelo —
"Mama, why wasn't David circumcised?"

Miriam Sud, 4 years old.
At Passover, Miriam asked her mother to give her a packet of Matzot for the kindergarten. Her mother said that it was not worth taking it to the kindergarten, better to take a little for the way. Miriam, calming herself, said:
"Yes, I suppose so. After all, when the Jews came out of Egypt, they took with them Matza for the journey. And so we Jews, too, should take some Matzah for the way."

Yana Teplitskaya, *8 years old, 7 years in refusal.*

41

Rina Fulmacht, *9 years old, 4 years in refusal.*

Finding out that children have milk teeth, Rina asked:

"But can one eat meat with milk teeth?"

Paul Praisman, 5 years old.

"I am certain that cats are not Jewish as they don't keep kosher."

Dimitry Vorobyev, *6 years old.*

"Mama, they compelled me to eat sausage meat. Will G-d punish me?

As when He sees a Jew, He always asks, 'Did you eat sausage meat?'"

42

Ilana Litvak, *3 years old, born in refusal.*

Ilana, having argued in the kindergarten with a boy, defiantly declared:

"Anyway, you don't know Shabbat songs!"

Mark Yuzefovich, 4 years old.
"Rain, rain, do not fall because I'm only a Jewish boy!"

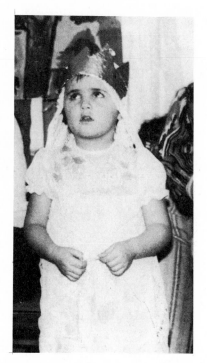

Judith Khasina, *9 years old, born in refusal.*

Mark Gurvich, 3 years old.

"Mama, what is that thing Israel?"

"That's a country where Jews live and speak Hebrew."

After sometime, they arrived at Misha Nudler's home. There were only Jews; and only Hebrew was being spoken. Mark said,

"I know, we have already arrived in Israel!"

Mark Gurvich, *8 years old.*
When Mark was five or six months old, he was in his cot and muttered,

"A – ba – ba."

"Aba ba."

His father was happy; his son had spoken his first words and straight away in Hebrew. (Aba ba in Hebrew means, "Father is coming!")

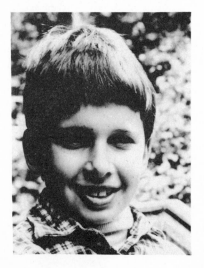

Kolya Z., *9 years old*

Having returned from a pioneer camp, summed up the situation there.

"My Jewish friends are 100 centuries cleverer than all those I met there."

Joseph Gurvich

"What language did Adam speak?"

His brother, Mark, answered, "Hebrew, of course. After all, G-d speaks Hebrew!"

Mitya Klotz, *8 years old, 5 years in* *refusal.*

Mark Yuzefovich, 2.5 years old.

A boy in the yard:

"You don't have a locomotive train!"

Mark: "But all the same, I am a Jew!"

45

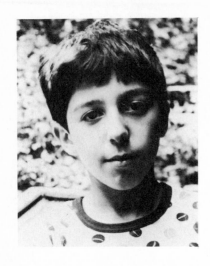

Simcha Sorin, *11 years old, 4 years in refusal.*

Mark Gurvich, 2.5 years old.
"Eifo my boots' aim?" ("Eifo" is "where" in Hebrew. "aim" is the Hebrew dual plural.)

Rita Litvak, *13 years old, 5 years in refusal.*

46

Michael K., 3 years old, after the arrival of the KGB at the Kindergarten:

"Papa, do you like policemen?"

"Yes."

"And I don't!"

Miriam Sud.

The first word in Hebrew which Miriam Sud said was "Shalom." Miriam mastered it well and always only greeted with this word bearded men who came to their home. But suddenly it was discovered that this word had a totally different meaning for her. One day when a friend arrived at their place, Miriam gleefully exclaimed,

"Mama, Shalom has arrived!"

And when, after him, another person entered, "Another shalom has arrived!"

Naomi Rakhlenko, 4½years old, born in refusal.

Under the influence of the Passover Haggadah, she asked,

"Mama, isn't it upon those people who don't allow us into grandma's flat that G-d will send the plague of locusts?"

Mark Gurvich, 6 years old.
"Where's the orange from?"
"From Greece."
"Is it possible to go there?"
"Yes it is."
"Then, is Greece part of the Soviet Union?"

Dina Yoffe, 7 years old.
"Mama, shhhhh. You shouldn't say anything aloud about our affairs."
"Why?"
"Because Busya said that they have put these things everywhere (pointing to the ceiling) and everything is being listened to."

Ilyusha Yakobson, *9 years old, 6 years in refusal.*

Mark Gurvich, 5 years old.

In the theatre, he says out loud to the whole hall:

"And in Israel, they don't show children such bad performances!"

Dina Yoffe, 7 years old.

In a conversation with a curious neighbor in the yard:

"I'm leaving soon for Eretz Yisrael, as it's my homeland."

"How will you live there? You don't even know the language."

"Yes, I do."

"Where did you learn it?"

"Ah, that's a secret which my mother told me never to reveal to anyone under any circumstances."

After the conversation, at home:

Mother: "Why didn't you say that your mother taught you?"

Dina: "Because then she would have asked who taught mama, and anyhow, it's forbidden to say."

Katya Razgon, *4 years old, recently in refusal.*

All data under children's photos conforms to their present age. Whereas the children's remarks may relate to an earlier age.   49

★ ★ ★

We gave several questions to mother-refuseniks and below we reprint their answers.

1. How many children have you and what are their ages?

Leah Chernobilsky: Three children. Anna – 14, Evgeny – 11, Yosef – 5 months.

Zoya Kopelman: I have two daughters: Aviya, born in 1978 and Dina, born in 1979.

2. Do they know that they are Jews? What do they understand by this?

Leah Chernobilsky: "Questions of Judaism, of all kinds of Jewish problems as well as episodes from Jewish history serve in our family as a constant theme of conversation and, in my opinion, form an integral part of our spiritual life. Since we have already been in refusal for ten years now, our children understand their Judaism as something natural and positive. Our stay in the Soviet Union is for them a sad result of a two thousand-year expulsion, and the most natural way out is to return to the homeland, Eretz-Yisrael. This natural form of Zionism of our children is actively exercised on grandmothers, grandfathers and other assimilated relatives, convincing them, albeit at present unsuccessfully, that the best way out of all the problems is to return to Eretz Yisrael."

Zoya Kopelman: 'From their very birth, they know that they are Jews, that is to say, that they belong to a special and ancient people, with whom G-d made an agreement, and to whom He gave the responsibility of fulfilling the Mitzvot. Moreover, they know that for a
50   long time, Jews did not have a homeland, but now there is one. Using

common sense and comparing family life with the surrounding world, my elder daughter had already at age 5½come independently to the conclusion that it would be far better and easier for us to live in Eretz Yisrael.

3. Do Your Children Know that the Family is in Refusal? Do They Somehow or Another Comment on this Situation?

Leah Chernobilsky: "Our children have more than once accompanied their friends who received permission to the airport on their way to Israel. At first, they tried to find some logic in the system of handing out permission. That is, whoever applied first was the first to leave. Unfortunately, we all were quickly shown that there is no logic and that one might have to wait a long time. To the question why we are refused permission to leave, we try to answer our children openly, and explain how we ourselves understand the problem. In our opinion, this is the only way to ensure that our children stay our friends. Any 'lie' to sqve things between close friends will only later lead to misunderstandings."

Zoya Kopelman: "Yes, our children know that we are refused permission to leave for Israel. This hangs over them and creates a permanent feeling of an absence of freedom. This occurs just at the time when our efforts are to raise them to be independent, freedom-loving people."

4. Do Your Children Study Hebrew? Do You Tell Them about the History of the Jewish People? Do You Celebrate Jewish Festivals in the Family?

Leah Chernobilsky: "Our children study Hebrew. We try to celebrate Jewish festivals together with friends – refuseniks who also have children around the same age as ours. Mixing with children who have the same ideals, dreams and problems, the children experience a wonderful feeling of solidarity and Jewish togetherness."

Zoya Kopelman: "Yes, my children study Hebrew. They love to insert Hebrew words and expressions into Russian conversations, and to sing songs in Hebrew. We tell them about the history of the Jewish people and celebrate all the Jewish Festivals for which the children wait with great expectation. Even their birthdays are celebrated according to the Jewish calendar: Tu B'Shvat for Aviya and the last day of Chanukah for Dina."

5. How Do Your Children Adapt to the State's Children's Institutions (Kindergartens, Schools, etc.?)

Leah Chernobilsky: "Our children have to go to school after a spell in our independent Jewish Kindergarten where we raise them with a pride in their Judaism, an independence of thought, initiative and where we share with them the dream of living in Eretz Yisrael. In the Soviet school, Israel is insulted, termed racist and fascist, an aggressor and so on. All of this anti-Zionism openly smells of anti-Semitism. For our children, hatred of Israel means a hatred of themselves as well. Therefore, the obligation of sending children to the State school is, in our opinion, one of the most difficult sides of refusenik life. Our children feel completely alien. They know that to admit their Zionism means undergoing instant oppression and insult. Every teacher is professionally obligated to censure Israel and Zionists and the schoolchildren soak up this attitude from the teachers. Therefore, our children can only mix with their classmates on a very superficial level. Their real friends are brother/sister refuseniks and Zionists all over the world. Unfortunately in Moscow, the refusenik families live in different areas and it is difficult for the children to spend time with their fellow Jews. But we try to help out in this respect."

Zoya Kopelman: "My children don't go to school as yet, the elder will go in September. However, for two years already, they have been singing in the choir of 'The House of Culture,' in whose repertoire there are many patriotic and pioneer songs. Despite the fact that both girls love to sing and love their choir-leader, they go to classes without a great deal of relish and they never participate in concerts on Soviet holidays. "We do not celebrate these holidays," they explain to me, but in the choir, they claim that they are too busy. My girls have not grown friendly with any of the children from the 'House of Culture', but in this environment, they feel their alienation even more strongly."

6. How Do the Children's Minds Cope with both the Official Propaganda and the Position Given to them by their Parents? Has There Arisen Any Conflict on this Point? And if so, what?

Leah Chernobilsky: "The official propaganda considers our children as something alien and has no dealings with them. We allow them to avoid answering ideological questions and to refuse to give answers in the lesson if the answers demanded from them do not conform with the world outlook of our children – even if it means a bad mark or calling the parents to the school. Unfortunately, because our children do not have the opportunity of not attending a government school, they cannot speak openly and freely about their views.

In order to protect them from a continual war with the teachers, we recommend that they act in a restrained fashion ("as we live here in a foreign country") and not to attract unnecessary hostility to oneself. I repeat that this situation is very difficult for the child – to go to school and hide his views there from everyone, and knowing that you are among potential enemies. From among their classmates today will be the Party workers, Ministry of Interior workers and KGB employees of tomorrow – the ideological oppressors of tomorrow who will not allow you to leave the USSR."

Zoya Kopelman: "I'll say straight away that I try to encourage in my children a tolerance and respect for the various world cultures, beliefs and habits that people have. In an attempt to spare the child's mind, I do not tell them that we live in a country of enemies. I try to teach them not to thrust their way thinking onto anyone else and not to pry into other people's lives. Thereby, as a rule, the children do not allow themselves to get involved in detailed discussions with neighbors or passers-by, but always bravely and quietly say that they are Jews. Although one year ago it seemed to them as if some pioneer children wanted to beat them up after such a declaration. My small girls were very frightened but somehow they got over it. As questions arise in reaction to Soviet radio, or headlines in the papers, or slogans and posters in the street, we do the best we can to try to explain in detail."

7. Were Your Children Witnesses to Searches, Arrests, Threats from the Police or KGB Agents? What was their Reaction?

Leah Chernobilsky: "Our children were many times witnesses to searches of flats and to the arrest of their father. They know when Boris hid from an unjustified trial; they knew when I went to the court and they did not sleep while they waited for me. They longed for their father when he was imprisoned. Many times I was forced to see the consequences of these impressions which weigh heavily on children's minds. My children awaken at night in tears, especially the elder girl. They are tormented by nightmares. They are persecuted in their sleep by KGB agents. My children are openly frightened of the police because these men broke down the door and turned the whole house upside down and then led their father away. If one of us is delayed in the evening and comes home late, the children are alarmed that we may have fallen into the clutches of the KGB. After all of this, can the children in school believe that there is a sunny childhood in the USSR "

Zoya Kopelman: "Thank G-d, my children have not seen searches, arrests. But persecution by the police when they tried to find out where their father worked, and the appearances every two or three days of local policemen at our flat with threats of parasitism — they experienced all this first-hand. They were then just five and three years old, and they now cannot see a policeman without fear and tears. Over a year has passed and much comforting and explaining were needed from my side before they learnt to view a policeman more or less calmly.

OUR CHILDREN'S CREATIVE WORKS

Naomi Drachinsky, 4½ years old, whilst this material was in preparation, received permission with her family to emigrate to Israel, where they now live.

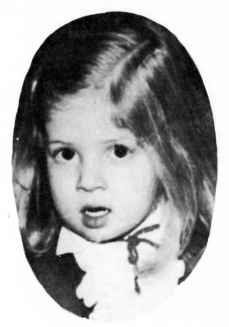

לפים לן, לפים, לן לפים
לן לפים,
לפים אנתקים,
לפים אנתקים,
מהרו, מהרו,
לפים אנתקים.

Miriam Yuzefovich, 9 years old.

ילדים לבנים שלהם.

פעם אחת בבית אחת היה ריב הבנים כי לבנה ברה
הבית ויבו היו הבנים פים מאלו ולריב הבנים היו כולו:
אחת אחת אמרה: "לא יפה, אבל הבנים".
‏– למה? – הבנים אחרים.
‏– כי – אמרה אחת – היפה – היפה לבנה אחד! רק
באחת כי היל כל רק היה לא לבכך אחד.
‏– לפה – אחת אחרים – כי לבלה אמרה אחת כל
היה. כאם אחרת שיא יהא אחת אחת.
‏– לא, אחרו אחת פרם לבנה לההת פרחים היתה,
אחר ילדים של מצייר ברם אחד יפה, אמרת אם
כילף כל ברבה בלו בכם בים יפים אמר.
‏– לא, אמרה ולפה לבנה לההת אמר אם בבך בוה
ולי אמיר אמר בוה.
אחר עקל כל הריב ודוו.
אחר לבנה ולבת בכפה אמר לאמרנו.
‏– אם קרה?
הבנים אחרו:
‏– כמאמר אחת יפם של אחת לההת אחת אלפם.
כל אמר?
‏– לא, אמרה לבנה, כי קפל של יבה אמר לא אחר בבך
שיבה לאנה יבה לכן היה אמו, ברה אל אחת לההת אל
החלק אבל הבנים.

56

Words of Mark Yuzefovich, 11 years old.

57

מנחם יוספי

מ יאמר עירו לירושלים
עירו לבלותה,
עירו כי אם על צא מ"מ
ותאמר תפלה...

נ יסים צעה ה" לבלותינו
ב'א'מ ההם בזמן הזה
כי בצאת ה" רועו
וכתנו בציון על

ח אם צצות
כי היו אוירו
כי לבלותינו, לבמההת
ותרי'עו בצירו

מ יאמר עירו לירושלים
עירו לבלותה
עירו כי אם על צא מ"מ
ותאמר תפלה...